DEALING WITH A NARCISSIST

Strategic Approaches for Dealing with Narcissistic or difficult people at Home and Workplace

Clinton Walton

temperamental
disinterested rigid tense
inflexible ???
florid
lewd joyless
WARNING
blundering
uncaring
desperate DEMENTIA
moody
reckless
tense
aggrieved
crude
anxious
rigid
gluttonous
paranoid frustrated
agitated
dismissive
irritable
unidimensional
erratic
irritable
distraught
impetuous
dismissive
heedless
offensive
crude
rash
joyless
impulsive
intrusive delusional
SIGNS OF
lewd ???
compulsive suspicious heedless unrealistic
argumentative
stubborn
anxious

Table of contents

INTRODUCTION

Dealing with a narcissist can be a challenging and intricate journey that often requires a delicate balance of understanding, resilience, and self-preservation. Narcissistic individuals, characterized by an excessive sense of self-importance and a lack of empathy, can create tumultuous relationships that leave others feeling emotionally drained and manipulated. This introduction explores the complexities of navigating such relationships, offering insights into the traits of narcissism, the impact on those involved, and strategies for coping and maintaining one's well-being.

At its core, narcissism is a personality trait marked by an inflated self-image, an insatiable need for admiration, and a lack of genuine empathy for others. While everyone may exhibit narcissistic tendencies to some extent, it becomes a personality disorder when these traits significantly impair social and interpersonal functioning. Narcissists often have an exaggerated sense of entitlement, a constant desire for attention, and a tendency to exploit others to achieve their own goals.

The Impact on Relationships:

Dealing with a narcissist in personal or professional relationships can be emotionally draining and psychologically taxing. The narcissistic individual may engage in manipulative behaviors such as gaslighting, where they distort reality to make their victims doubt their own perceptions. Additionally, they often display a lack of genuine interest in the needs and feelings of others, leading to a one-sided and unfulfilling dynamic.

In romantic relationships, a narcissist may initially present themselves as charming and attentive, drawing their partner in with flattery and grand gestures. However, over time, their need for constant admiration and lack of empathy can lead to a cycle of emotional abuse and instability. Friendships and professional partnerships with narcissists may also be marked by a constant power struggle and a pervasive sense of walking on eggshells.

Coping Strategies:

Navigating relationships with narcissists requires a multifaceted approach that prioritizes self-care and emotional well-being. Establishing boundaries is crucial in protecting oneself from the manipulative tactics of a narcissist. Clearly communicating what is and isn't acceptable behavior can help create a healthier dynamic, although it may be met with resistance.

Maintaining a strong support system is another vital aspect of coping with a narcissist. Seeking guidance from friends, family, or mental health professionals can provide perspective and validation for those dealing with the challenges of these relationships. It's essential to remember that the behavior of a narcissist is not a reflection of the victim's worth or value.

Additionally, developing and maintaining a sense of self is crucial when entangled with a narcissist. Often, the constant focus on the needs and desires of the narcissistic individual can lead to a loss of one's identity. Engaging in activities that bring joy and fulfillment, pursuing personal goals, and practicing self-compassion are vital components of preserving one's sense of self in the midst of a challenging relationship.

Exit Strategies:
In some cases, the toxicity of a relationship with a narcissist may become untenable, necessitating the consideration of exit strategies. Ending a relationship with a narcissist can be a complex process, as it often involves overcoming emotional attachment and potential backlash from the narcissistic individual. Seeking professional guidance, such as therapy or counseling, can provide valuable support and guidance during this challenging period.

It's important to note that exiting a relationship with a narcissist may not necessarily lead to immediate relief. Narcissists may resist the end of the relationship, employing tactics such as guilt-tripping, manipulation, or attempts to regain control. Staying resolute and maintaining support from friends, family, or professionals is crucial during this vulnerable time.

Dealing with a narcissist is a complex and nuanced experience that requires a combination of self-awareness, resilience, and external support. Understanding the traits of narcissism, recognizing its impact on relationships, and implementing effective coping strategies are essential components of navigating these challenging dynamics. While the journey may be arduous, prioritizing one's well-being and seeking professional guidance when needed can ultimately lead to personal growth and healing in the aftermath of a relationship with a narcissist.

Chapter One

Understanding Narcissism

Definition and Traits

Definition of Narcissism:
Narcissism is a personality trait characterized by a pervasive pattern of grandiosity, a constant need for admiration, and a lack of empathy towards others. Individuals with narcissistic traits often exhibit an exaggerated sense of self-importance, a preoccupation with fantasies of unlimited success, power, brilliance, beauty, or ideal love.

Key Traits of Narcissism:

Grandiosity: Narcissists possess an inflated sense of self-worth, believing they are unique and superior to others. This often leads to a preoccupation with fantasies of unlimited success, power, or beauty.

Need for Admiration: Individuals with narcissistic traits constantly seek excessive admiration from others to reinforce their sense of self-importance. They are often preoccupied with their own achievements and require constant validation.

Lack of Empathy: Empathy, the ability to understand and share the feelings of others, is notably lacking in narcissistic individuals. They may struggle to recognize or acknowledge the emotions and needs of those around them.

Sense of Entitlement: Narcissists often believe they are entitled to special treatment and expect favorable treatment without considering the needs or feelings of others.

Exploitative Behavior: Some narcissists display a pattern of taking advantage of others to achieve their own goals. They may exploit relationships or manipulate situations to serve their own interests.

Envy and Jealousy: Narcissistic individuals may harbor envy and jealousy towards others, particularly those perceived as threats or rivals. This can lead to a competitive and hostile attitude.

Arrogance: Arrogance and haughty behaviors are common in narcissists. They may belittle or look down upon others whom they perceive as inferior.

Understanding narcissism involves recognizing the complex interplay of these traits, which can vary in intensity and expression among individuals. It's essential to approach this understanding with sensitivity and an awareness of the potential impact on interpersonal relationships.

Types of Narcissistic Personality Disorder (NPD)

Narcissistic Personality Disorder is a clinical diagnosis in the Diagnostic and Statistical Manual of Mental Disorders (DSM-5), and it encompasses several subtypes or manifestations. It's important to note that individuals with NPD may exhibit a combination of these traits, and not every narcissist fits neatly into a single subtype. Here are some common types:

Grandiose Narcissist:
Characterized by an overt display of grandiosity, these individuals exhibit an exaggerated sense of self-importance and superiority.
They often seek constant admiration, have a sense of entitlement, and may be preoccupied with fantasies of unlimited success, power, or beauty.

Vulnerable Narcissist:
Contrary to the overt grandiosity of the grandiose narcissist, the vulnerable narcissist presents as more fragile and defensive.
They may be hypersensitive to criticism, experience chronic feelings of inadequacy, and use a façade of superiority to mask deep-seated insecurities.

Malignant Narcissist:
Combining traits of NPD with antisocial behavior, the malignant narcissist can be manipulative, deceitful, and even sadistic.
They may engage in harmful behaviors without remorse, exploit others for personal gain, and lack empathy to an extreme degree.

Cerebral Narcissist:
This subtype focuses on intellectual achievements and prowess to bolster their sense of superiority.
They may be highly knowledgeable in specific areas and use their intelligence as a tool for manipulation or control.

Somatic Narcissist:
In contrast to the cerebral narcissist, the somatic narcissist seeks validation through physical appearance and sexual conquests.
They often emphasize their attractiveness and may use their physical appearance to gain attention and admiration.

Collective Narcissist:

While not officially recognized in the DSM-5, some researchers discuss the concept of collective narcissism, where individuals identify with a group (such as a nation or community) and demand excessive admiration for that group.

This can manifest as an extreme patriotism or group superiority complex.

Understanding these subtypes helps to grasp the diversity within narcissistic personalities. It's crucial to approach individuals with NPD with empathy while recognizing the challenges they face in forming healthy relationships and understanding the impact their behavior may have on themselves and others.

Chapter Two

Recognizing Narcissistic Behavior

Common Signs and Red Flags

I. **Exaggerated Self-Importance:**
Narcissists often display an inflated sense of their own achievements and talents, exaggerating their importance in various aspects of life.

II. **Preoccupation with Fantasies of Unlimited Success, Power, Brilliance, or Beauty:**
They may indulge in grandiose fantasies, believing they are destined for exceptional success or recognition, even if not supported by reality.

III. **Belief in their Uniqueness and Need for Special Treatment:**
Narcissists tend to see themselves as unique individuals who deserve special privileges and are unwilling to associate with those they perceive as beneath them.

IV. **Sense of Entitlement:**
A key red flag is their expectation of special treatment without reciprocating, as they believe they are entitled to privileges and resources.

V. **Exploitative Behavior:**
Narcissists often take advantage of others to achieve their goals, lacking empathy for the impact their actions may have on those around them.

VI. **Lack of Empathy:**
Difficulty understanding or acknowledging the feelings of others, coupled with a lack of genuine concern for their well-being.

VII. **Envy of Others or Belief that Others Envy Them:**
Narcissists may envy others and simultaneously believe that others envy them, contributing to a constant need for validation and superiority.

VIII. **Arrogant and Haughty Behavior**:
Displaying a condescending attitude, arrogance, and a belief that they are inherently superior to others.

IX. **Frequent Requirement of Admiration**:
A continual need for praise and admiration from others to fuel their fragile self-esteem.

X. **Difficulty Handling Criticism:**
Narcissists often react negatively to criticism, becoming defensive, angry, or dismissive as they struggle with challenges to their perceived perfection.

XI. **Interpersonal Difficulties:**
Maintaining stable relationships can be challenging, as narcissists may struggle with genuine connection, using others as a means to fulfill their needs rather than fostering mutual understanding.

XII. **Boundary Violations:**
Crossing personal boundaries without regard for others' autonomy, reflecting a disregard for the rights and feelings of those around them. Recognizing these signs is crucial for identifying narcissistic behavior and understanding its impact on relationships and interactions.

Impact on Relationships and Interactions

I. **Dysfunctional Interpersonal Dynamics:**
Narcissistic behavior often leads to dysfunctional relationships, characterized by a lack of genuine emotional connection and reciprocity. The focus on the narcissist's needs can overshadow the needs of others, creating an imbalanced dynamic.

II. Emotional Manipulation:

Narcissists may employ emotional manipulation tactics to control and exploit others. This can include guilt-tripping, gaslighting, or using charm to gain compliance.

III. Difficulty in Resolving Conflict:

Due to a narcissist's inability to handle criticism and their inclination to deflect blame, conflicts within relationships can escalate without resolution. Healthy communication becomes challenging.

IV. Erosion of Self-Esteem in Others:

Constant need for admiration and superiority can lead narcissists to belittle others. Over time, this can erode the self-esteem of those in their orbit, as they may feel devalued and unimportant.

V. Isolation of Others:

Narcissists may isolate individuals in their lives, strategically limiting their connections to maintain control. This isolation can lead to a dependence on the narcissist and further amplify their perceived importance.

VI. Cycle of Idealization and Devaluation:

Relationships with narcissists often follow a cycle of idealization, where the individual is initially put on a pedestal, followed by devaluation when the narcissist's unrealistic expectations are not met.

This cycle can be emotionally exhausting for those involved.

VII. **Impact on Professional Relationships:**
In the workplace, narcissistic behavior can hinder collaboration and teamwork. Colleagues may feel overshadowed, undermined, or manipulated, affecting overall productivity and morale.

VIII. **Parental Impact on Children:**
Narcissistic parents may exhibit favoritism, using children as extensions of themselves. This can lead to emotional neglect, as the child's needs and identity are subordinated to the narcissistic parent's desires.

IX. **Inability to Nurture Healthy Relationships:**
The self-centered nature of narcissistic individuals often impedes their ability to foster mutually supportive and fulfilling relationships. Genuine emotional intimacy becomes challenging to achieve.

X. **Long-Term Consequences:**
Sustained exposure to narcissistic behavior can result in lasting emotional scars, impacting individuals' trust, self-worth, and ability to form healthy connections in the future.
Understanding the profound impact of narcissistic behavior on relationships and interactions is crucial for individuals dealing with such dynamics,

providing a foundation for setting boundaries and seeking support for personal growth and healing.

Chapter Three

Strategies for Dealing with a Narcissist

Setting Boundaries

Setting boundaries with a narcissist can be a delicate yet crucial aspect of maintaining your well-being and managing relationships effectively. Narcissistic individuals often exhibit patterns of entitlement, manipulation, and a lack of empathy, making it essential to establish clear limits to protect yourself emotionally. In navigating this complex terrain, several strategies can prove helpful.

1. **Define Your Boundaries:**
Begin by identifying your own needs and limits. Reflect on what behaviors you find unacceptable and the emotional toll they may take. Establishing clarity within yourself is the foundation for effectively communicating boundaries to the narcissist.

2. **Communicate Assertively:**

When expressing your boundaries, use assertive communication. Clearly state your needs without aggression or passivity. Be specific about the behaviors you find problematic, focusing on concrete examples to avoid ambiguity.

3. **Be Consistent:**

Consistency is key when dealing with narcissists. Enforce your boundaries consistently, as any perceived inconsistency may be exploited by a narcissist seeking to test or challenge them. Stand firm, even in the face of manipulation or guilt-tripping.

4. **Avoid JADE (Justify, Argue, Defend, Explain):**

Narcissists often thrive on engaging in power struggles and attempting to undermine your boundaries. Refrain from justifying, arguing, defending, or explaining your boundaries excessively. Keep your responses brief and clear to avoid being drawn into emotional battles.

5. **Limit Emotional Engagement:**

Maintain emotional distance when necessary. Narcissists may provoke emotional reactions to maintain control. By limiting your emotional engagement, you reduce their ability to manipulate and drain your energy.

6. **Seek Support**:
Building a support network is crucial. Share your experiences with trustworthy friends, family, or therapists who can provide guidance and emotional support. Narcissists may attempt to isolate individuals, so maintaining connections is vital.

7. **Practice Self-Care:**
Prioritize self-care to bolster your emotional resilience. Narcissistic relationships can be draining, so ensure you engage in activities that promote mental and physical well-being. This might include exercise, hobbies, and taking time for yourself.

8. **Consider Professional Help:**
If the relationship becomes particularly challenging, seeking the assistance of a therapist or counselor can provide valuable insights and coping strategies. A professional can help you navigate the complexities of dealing with a narcissist and offer guidance tailored to your situation.

9. **Know When to Walk Away:**
In some cases, despite your best efforts, a relationship with a narcissist may be toxic and irreparable. Knowing when to walk away is a difficult but crucial decision for your mental health. Prioritize your well-being over the desire to change someone who may be resistant to change.

10. **Set Consequences:**
Clearly communicate the consequences of crossing boundaries. Whether it's limiting contact, taking a break, or ending the relationship, setting consequences reinforces the importance of respecting your boundaries.

In conclusion, setting boundaries with a narcissist is a multifaceted process that requires self-awareness, assertiveness, and resilience. By defining and communicating your limits consistently, seeking support, practicing self-care, and, when necessary, considering professional help, you can navigate these challenging relationships more effectively while safeguarding your own emotional health.

Communication Techniques

Effective communication with a narcissist necessitates a nuanced approach, considering their propensity for manipulation and self-centeredness. Employing specific techniques can enhance your ability to convey messages clearly, minimize conflict, and maintain a semblance of balance in your interactions.

1. Use "I" Statements:
Frame your statements using "I" rather than "you" to express your feelings and needs. This reduces the likelihood of the narcissist feeling attacked or

becoming defensive. For instance, say, "I feel upset when..." instead of "You always make me upset."

2. Stay Calm and Collected:
Maintain a calm demeanor, even in the face of provocation. Narcissists may attempt to elicit emotional reactions for control. By remaining composed, you limit their ability to manipulate your emotions.

3. Be Clear and Specific:
Avoid vague or ambiguous language. Clearly articulate your thoughts and expectations, providing concrete examples when necessary. Narcissists may exploit ambiguity to reinterpret messages in their favor.

4. Set Realistic Expectations:
Recognize that a narcissist may not be capable of genuine empathy or understanding. Adjust your expectations accordingly, focusing on conveying information rather than expecting an emotional response.

5. Choose Your Battles:
Not every issue requires confrontation. Prioritize your concerns and address only the most important ones. This helps in conserving energy and maintaining a more strategic approach to communication.

6. Practice Active Listening:
Demonstrate that you are listening attentively by summarizing what the narcissist has said and asking clarifying questions. This can create a more constructive dialogue and convey your willingness to engage in a meaningful conversation.

7. Use Positive Reinforcement:
Acknowledge positive behaviors or moments of cooperation. Positive reinforcement can encourage more favorable interactions, although it may not fundamentally alter narcissistic tendencies.

8. Avoid Jargon or Complex Language:
Keep your language simple and straightforward. Narcissists may exploit confusion to assert control. Clarity minimizes the chance of misinterpretation.

9. Stay Grounded in Reality:
Narcissists may distort facts to suit their narrative. Counteract this by consistently presenting objective information and relying on evidence when discussing specific incidents.

10. Establish and Enforce Consequences:
Clearly communicate the consequences of non-compliance or disrespectful behavior. This adds a practical dimension to your communication, emphasizing the importance of mutual respect.

11. Be Prepared to Disengage:
Recognize when a conversation is becoming unproductive or emotionally draining. It is sometimes necessary to disengage to protect your well-being. Set boundaries around when and how you engage in communication.

12. Seek Feedback:
Encourage open communication by inviting feedback. This can create an environment where both parties feel heard and understood, fostering a more collaborative dynamic.

In summary, effective communication with a narcissist involves maintaining composure, clarity, and strategic engagement. By utilizing "I" statements, setting realistic expectations, and choosing your battles wisely, you can navigate conversations more successfully while mitigating potential conflicts inherent in dealing with narcissistic individuals.

Self-Care and Emotional Well-being

Self-care is paramount when dealing with a narcissist, as these relationships can be emotionally taxing and challenging. Prioritizing your well-being is essential to maintain resilience, foster emotional health, and navigate the complexities of interacting with a narcissistic individual.

1. Establish Healthy Boundaries:
Set clear and firm boundaries to protect your emotional space. Recognize your limits and communicate them assertively. This includes limiting exposure to toxic behaviors and knowing when to step back for self-preservation.

2. Nurture Supportive Relationships:
Develop connections with family, friends, or support networks that are aware of your circumstances. Having a reliable support network is crucial for emotional validation, advice, and encouragement.

3. Practice Mindfulness and Stress Reduction:
Incorporate mindfulness practices into your everyday routine, such as deep breathing and meditation. These practices can help manage stress, increase self-awareness, and enhance your ability to stay grounded in challenging situations.

4. Engage in Regular Exercise:
Physical activity is a powerful tool for emotional well-being. Regular exercise releases endorphins, which can improve mood and reduce stress. Choose activities you enjoy to make it a sustainable part of your routine.

5. Pursue Hobbies and Activities:
Nurture your interests and engage in activities that bring you joy. This not only provides an outlet for self-expression but also offers a healthy distraction from the challenges of dealing with a narcissist.

6. Prioritize Self-Reflection:
Regularly reflect on your emotions and experiences. Journaling can be a valuable tool for processing thoughts and emotions, helping you gain clarity and insight into your own needs and reactions.

7. Set Realistic Expectations:
Accept that you cannot change the narcissist's behavior. Adjust your expectations to focus on what you can control—your responses, boundaries, and well-being. This realistic perspective can alleviate frustration and disappointment.

8. Seek Professional Support:
Therapy or counseling can be instrumental in navigating the emotional complexities of dealing with a narcissist. A mental health professional can provide guidance, coping strategies, and a safe space to explore your feelings.

9. Practice Self-Compassion:
Be kind to yourself. Recognize that dealing with a narcissist can be challenging, and it's okay to prioritize your own needs. Practice self-compassion

by treating yourself with the same kindness you would offer a friend facing similar difficulties.

10. Establish a Self-Care Routine:
Create a routine that incorporates self-care activities. Whether it's a warm bath, reading a book, or taking a walk, having dedicated time for self-care reinforces the importance of nurturing your well-being.

11. Learn and Use Stress Management Techniques:
Explore various stress management techniques, such as progressive muscle relaxation, guided imagery, or aromatherapy. These tools can be effective in reducing stress and promoting emotional balance.

12. Celebrate Small Achievements: No matter how tiny, acknowledge and celebrate your victories. Recognizing your resilience and growth reinforces a positive self-image and boosts your emotional well-being.

In conclusion, prioritizing self-care and emotional well-being is crucial when navigating relationships with narcissistic individuals. Establishing boundaries, seeking support, practicing mindfulness, and engaging in activities that bring joy contribute to a resilient and balanced emotional state, empowering you to cope with the challenges inherent in such relationships.

Chapter Four

Coping Mechanisms

Seeking Support from Others

Coping with a narcissist can be a challenging and emotionally draining experience. One effective strategy is seeking support from others, as it provides a crucial foundation for emotional resilience and understanding. In navigating this complex terrain, individuals often find solace and guidance through interpersonal connections.

Isolation is a common tactic employed by narcissists to maintain control, making external support invaluable. When facing the manipulative tendencies of a narcissist, confiding in friends, family, or support groups becomes a vital coping mechanism. These connections offer a reality check, validating the victim's experiences and feelings, which may be consistently undermined by the narcissist.

Sharing experiences with others provides an external perspective that helps individuals recognize and articulate the manipulative behaviors they may be subjected to. Friends and family become a sounding board, aiding in the validation of emotions and the identification of patterns characteristic of narcissistic relationships. This validation is pivotal for individuals who often doubt their own perceptions due to the gaslighting commonly associated with narcissistic behavior.

Furthermore, seeking support serves as an emotional anchor during tumultuous times. The empathetic presence of friends or support groups fosters a sense of belonging and understanding. This emotional connection acts as a buffer against the psychological impact of interacting with a narcissist, preventing feelings of isolation and despair.

In addition to emotional support, practical advice from others who have navigated similar situations can be invaluable. Friends or support groups may share coping strategies, enabling individuals to develop a repertoire of effective responses to narcissistic behaviors. These shared insights empower individuals to set boundaries, assert themselves, and regain a sense of control in the relationship.

An often-overlooked aspect of seeking support is the role of professional help. Therapists, counselors, or support hotlines can offer specialized guidance tailored to the nuances of dealing with a narcissist. Professional intervention equips individuals with coping mechanisms, enhances their emotional resilience, and provides a structured environment for processing and healing.

While seeking support from others is a potent coping mechanism, it's essential to approach it with discernment. Selecting confidants who are understanding and non-judgmental is crucial. Opening up to those who may inadvertently perpetuate blame or skepticism can exacerbate feelings of vulnerability and isolation.
Seeking support from others is a multifaceted and essential coping mechanism when dealing with a narcissist. Emotional validation, external perspectives, and practical advice form a robust support system that counteracts the isolating tactics employed by narcissists. Whether through friends, family, support groups, or professional help, building a network of understanding individuals provides the foundation for resilience, empowerment, and ultimately, breaking free from the emotional clutches of a narcissistic relationship.

Professional Help and Counseling

Professional help and counseling play a pivotal role in navigating the complexities of dealing with a narcissist. In the realm of coping mechanisms, seeking the expertise of mental health professionals offers a structured and specialized approach to address the unique challenges posed by narcissistic relationships.

One of the primary benefits of professional help is the objective perspective that therapists and counselors bring to the table. These professionals are trained to analyze interpersonal dynamics, recognize patterns of manipulation, and provide insights that may be obscured by the emotional entanglement of the relationship. Their impartiality is crucial in helping individuals gain clarity about the dynamics at play and empowering them to make informed decisions.

Therapists also assist individuals in understanding the impact of narcissistic behavior on their mental and emotional well-being. By exploring the emotional toll of the relationship, individuals can begin to untangle themselves from the web of manipulation and gaslighting. This self-awareness is a key step towards building resilience and reclaiming a sense of identity that may have been eroded by the narcissist's tactics.

Moreover, therapy provides a safe and confidential space for individuals to express their thoughts and feelings without fear of judgment. This is particularly important in narcissistic relationships where victims may experience isolation and self-doubt. The therapeutic environment becomes a sanctuary for validation, allowing individuals to articulate their experiences and emotions without the fear of dismissal or ridicule.

Counselors and therapists also work with individuals to develop coping strategies tailored to their specific situation. These strategies may include setting boundaries, assertiveness training, and learning effective communication skills. The goal is to empower individuals to navigate the challenges posed by the narcissist, ultimately fostering a greater sense of control and autonomy.

In cases where the narcissistic relationship has led to significant emotional trauma, therapeutic interventions such as trauma-focused therapy may be recommended. This specialized approach helps individuals process and heal from the psychological wounds inflicted by the narcissist, promoting long-term emotional well-being.

Additionally, therapists can assist in developing exit strategies for those looking to disengage from a narcissistic relationship. They offer guidance on planning a safe departure, managing potential backlash, and rebuilding one's life post-relationship.

This comprehensive support is invaluable for individuals seeking to break free from the toxic cycle of a narcissistic dynamic.

In conclusion, professional help and counseling form a crucial pillar in the arsenal of coping mechanisms for dealing with a narcissist. Therapists and counselors bring objectivity, expertise, and tailored interventions to empower individuals, facilitate healing, and guide them towards reclaiming their emotional well-being. The collaborative journey with a mental health professional is a transformative process that equips individuals with the tools and resilience needed to navigate the challenges posed by narcissistic relationships.

Developing Resilience

Developing resilience is a key coping mechanism when dealing with a narcissist, as it empowers individuals to navigate the emotional challenges and uncertainties inherent in such relationships. Resilience involves cultivating the ability to bounce back from adversity, adapt to changing circumstances, and maintain a sense of well-being despite the presence of a narcissistic individual.

One fundamental aspect of building resilience is self-awareness. Understanding one's emotions, triggers, and vulnerabilities provides a solid foundation for developing coping strategies. Recognizing the impact of the narcissistic relationship on mental and emotional well-being allows individuals to proactively address their needs and prioritize self-care.

Setting and maintaining boundaries is a crucial component of resilience. Narcissists often push boundaries and manipulate others to suit their needs. Learning to assertively communicate and defend personal boundaries is empowering, fostering a sense of control and self-efficacy. This process involves recognizing that it is acceptable to prioritize one's well-being and say no to manipulative behaviors.

Cultivating a support network is another vital element in building resilience. Connecting with understanding friends, family, or support groups creates a sense of community and validation. Sharing experiences and coping strategies with others who have faced similar challenges fosters a collective strength that reinforces individual resilience. The support network becomes a source of encouragement during difficult times and provides perspectives that counteract the gaslighting often associated with narcissistic relationships.

In addition to external support, developing internal resilience involves cultivating a positive mindset. This includes reframing negative thoughts, focusing on strengths, and finding silver linings in challenging situations. Building a reservoir of positive emotions contributes to emotional well-being and enhances the ability to weather the storm of a narcissistic relationship.

Mindfulness practices, such as meditation and deep breathing exercises, are effective tools for developing resilience. These practices help individuals stay grounded in the present moment, reducing anxiety about past events or future uncertainties. Mindfulness fosters emotional regulation, allowing individuals to respond to narcissistic behaviors with composure and clarity.

Taking care of physical health is integral to overall resilience. Regular exercise, proper nutrition, and sufficient sleep contribute to mental and emotional well-being. Physical well-being provides a solid foundation for facing the challenges posed by a narcissistic relationship, enhancing one's ability to cope with stress and maintain emotional balance.

Lastly, seeking professional help, such as therapy or counseling, can be instrumental in developing resilience. Therapists can provide guidance on building coping strategies, managing stress, and fostering emotional strength. The therapeutic relationship becomes a supportive anchor, assisting individuals in their journey towards greater resilience and well-being.

In conclusion, developing resilience is a multifaceted and dynamic process that empowers individuals to navigate the complexities of dealing with a narcissist. Through self-awareness, setting boundaries, cultivating a support network, maintaining a positive mindset, practicing mindfulness, and prioritizing physical health, individuals can build the emotional strength needed to withstand the challenges of narcissistic relationships. This resilience not only facilitates coping but also serves as a foundation for reclaiming personal agency and well-being in the face of adversity.

Chapter Five

Navigating Specific Relationships

Dealing with a Narcissistic Partner

Navigating a relationship with a narcissistic partner can be a complex and challenging journey, requiring a delicate balance of self-care, empathy, and assertiveness. Understanding the characteristics of narcissism is crucial in developing strategies to cope with the dynamics inherent in such relationships.

Narcissistic individuals often exhibit a grandiose sense of self-importance, a preoccupation with fantasies of unlimited success, and a lack of empathy for others. In the context of a romantic relationship, these traits can manifest in manipulative behaviors, a constant need for admiration, and a tendency to exploit others for personal gain.

One key aspect of dealing with a narcissistic partner is establishing and maintaining clear boundaries. Narcissists may push these boundaries to test their limits, so it is essential to communicate assertively and consistently. This involves expressing your needs and expectations while firmly standing your ground when faced with manipulation or disregard for your feelings.

Maintaining a strong sense of self is paramount when navigating a relationship with a narcissistic partner. It's easy to get entangled in their web of self-centeredness, but holding onto your identity and values will help you resist being constantly swayed by their desires. Self-reflection and self-care become crucial tools for preserving your mental and emotional well-being.

Effective communication is another vital component. Narcissists often struggle with genuine empathy, so expressing your feelings in a clear and non-confrontational manner can be challenging. Focus on "I" statements to convey your emotions without placing blame, creating an opportunity for your partner to better understand your perspective.

Educate yourself about narcissism to gain insight into your partner's behavior. Recognizing that their actions are rooted in their personality disorder can provide a degree of detachment, allowing you to respond more objectively. However, it's essential to balance understanding with the acknowledgment that their behavior is not an excuse for mistreatment.

Seeking professional help, such as couples therapy or individual counseling, can be instrumental in navigating the complexities of a relationship with a narcissistic partner. A therapist can provide guidance, facilitate communication, and assist in developing coping strategies tailored to your specific situation.

When dealing with a narcissistic partner, it's crucial to set realistic expectations. Changing the core traits of a narcissistic individual is challenging, and expecting them to suddenly become more empathetic or self-aware may lead to disappointment. Focus on managing the impact their behavior has on you and explore ways to cope with the challenges inherent in the relationship.

In conclusion, navigating a relationship with a narcissistic partner requires a multifaceted approach. Establishing clear boundaries, maintaining a strong sense of self, effective communication, education, and seeking professional help are essential components of managing the complexities inherent in such relationships. Remember that self-care is paramount, and understanding the nature of narcissism can empower you to make informed decisions about the future of the relationship.

Coping with a Narcissistic Family Member

Coping with a narcissistic family member can be an emotionally taxing experience, as the dynamics within a family setting can be uniquely complex. Whether dealing with a narcissistic parent, sibling, or other family member, understanding and implementing effective coping strategies is crucial for maintaining your well-being and preserving relationships.

1. Establish Boundaries:
Similar to dealing with a narcissistic partner, setting and maintaining clear boundaries is paramount. Narcissistic family members may attempt to manipulate or control those around them. Clearly communicate your limits and be firm in enforcing them, even if it requires distancing yourself emotionally or physically when necessary.

2. Practice Self-Care:
Caring for your own well-being becomes particularly important when dealing with a narcissistic family member. Engage in enjoyable and stress-relieving activities. Establish routines that prioritize your mental and physical health, creating a buffer against the emotional toll that interactions with a narcissist can take.

3. Develop a Support System:
Building a support network outside of the family is essential. Share your experiences with friends, seek advice from trusted individuals, or consider joining a support group. Connecting with others who have faced similar challenges can provide validation, understanding, and practical advice.

4. Maintain Realistic Expectations:
Understanding that you may not be able to change the narcissistic family member is crucial. Recognize the limitations of your influence and focus on managing your own responses and emotions. Unrealistic expectations can lead to disappointment and frustration, so adjusting them to align with the reality of the situation is essential.

5. Seek Professional Guidance:
Therapy, whether individual or family-oriented, can be a valuable resource. A mental health professional can provide insights into coping strategies, offer a safe space to explore your feelings, and guide you in developing effective communication techniques. Additionally, therapy can aid in setting healthy boundaries and understanding the impact of narcissistic behavior on family dynamics.

6. Develop Emotional Detachment:
While maintaining empathy for your family member, cultivating emotional detachment can help shield you from the negative effects of their behavior. This

doesn't mean shutting off emotions entirely but rather creating a psychological distance to protect your own mental well-being.

7. Reframe Your Perspective:
Try to reframe how you perceive and react to the narcissistic family member. Understand that their behavior is a reflection of their own insecurities and challenges rather than a judgment of your worth. This shift in perspective can empower you to respond with more compassion and less personal distress.

8. Focus on Communication:
When engaging with a narcissistic family member, effective communication becomes a key tool. Use assertive communication techniques, expressing your feelings and needs clearly while avoiding confrontations. Focus on "I" statements to convey your perspective without blaming or accusing, fostering a more open and constructive dialogue.

9. Set Realistic Boundaries for Involvement:
Evaluate the level of involvement you want with the narcissistic family member. While complete avoidance might not always be possible, establishing realistic boundaries for interaction can help manage stress and limit exposure to negative behaviors.

10. Cultivate Empathy for Yourself:
Finally, remember to extend empathy to yourself.
Dealing with a narcissistic family member can be
emotionally draining, and it's crucial to
acknowledge and validate your own feelings. Be
patient with yourself as you navigate these
challenging relationships.

Coping with a narcissistic family member requires a
combination of assertive communication, self-care,
realistic expectations, and, in some cases,
professional support. By establishing and
maintaining boundaries, practicing self-care,
developing a support system, and reframing your
perspective, you can navigate these complex
relationships with resilience and maintain your own
emotional well-being.

Handling Narcissistic Colleagues or Friends

Handling narcissistic colleagues or friends requires
a nuanced approach that balances professionalism,
self-preservation, and effective communication.
Whether in the workplace or social circles, dealing
with individuals exhibiting narcissistic traits can be
challenging, but with strategic coping strategies, it
is possible to navigate these relationships.

1. Maintain Professionalism:
In a workplace setting, maintaining a professional demeanor is crucial. Keep interactions focused on work-related matters and avoid being drawn into unnecessary personal drama. With friends, set clear boundaries to protect your emotional well-being.

2. Recognize Narcissistic Traits:
Understanding the traits associated with narcissism is a key step. Narcissistic individuals often display a sense of entitlement, a lack of empathy, and a constant need for admiration. Recognizing these behaviors allows you to approach interactions with a heightened awareness.

3. Limit Personal Sharing:
Be cautious about sharing personal information, especially vulnerabilities, with narcissistic colleagues or friends. They may use such information against you or manipulate it to serve their own agenda.

4. Set Boundaries Firmly:
Establish clear and firm boundaries in your interactions. Narcissistic individuals may push limits to test boundaries, so it's important to be consistent in enforcing them. Clearly communicate your expectations and be assertive in maintaining these boundaries.

5. Focus on Objective Communication:
When communicating with narcissistic colleagues or friends, keep discussions objective and task-oriented. Emphasize facts and avoid getting entangled in emotional arguments. This can help minimize potential conflicts and keep interactions more manageable.

6. Be Selective with Feedback:
If providing feedback, be selective and constructive. Narcissistic individuals may not respond well to criticism, so frame feedback in a way that highlights areas for improvement rather than pointing out flaws. Choose your battles wisely to maintain a more positive working or social environment.

7. Build Alliances:
In the workplace, consider building alliances with other colleagues who may share similar experiences. This can create a support system and provide a network for sharing insights and strategies for dealing with narcissistic behavior. In social circles, seek out friends who understand and support your boundaries.

8. Practice Emotional Detachment:
Cultivate emotional detachment to shield yourself from the emotional impact of narcissistic behavior. While empathy is important, maintaining a certain level of detachment can help you navigate interactions more objectively and protect your own mental well-being.

9. Stay Calm and Collected:
Narcissistic individuals may provoke emotional reactions, but it's essential to stay calm and collected. Responding emotionally may fuel their behavior, so maintain a composed demeanor in both professional and social interactions.

10. Know When to Seek Support:
If the challenges become overwhelming, know when to seek support from HR, a supervisor, or a trusted friend. Document specific instances of problematic behavior and approach the situation with a focus on finding constructive solutions.

11. Consider Professional Help:
If the situation escalates or significantly impacts your well-being, consider seeking professional help. Workplace counselors or therapists can provide guidance and coping strategies tailored to your specific situation.

Handling narcissistic colleagues or friends requires a combination of professionalism, assertiveness, and strategic communication. By recognizing narcissistic traits, setting firm boundaries, focusing on objective communication, and seeking support when necessary, you can navigate these relationships with resilience and maintain a healthy balance between your professional or social life and your well-being.

Chapter Six

Long-Term Considerations

Assessing the Relationship

Assessing a relationship with a narcissist requires a nuanced understanding of their behaviors, patterns, and the impact on your well-being. Recognizing the signs early on is crucial for navigating the complexities of dealing with a narcissist over the long term.

Narcissists often display a grandiose sense of self-importance, an insatiable need for admiration, and a lack of empathy. In assessing the relationship, observe how these traits manifest in your interactions. Consider instances where your achievements are overshadowed, or your emotions are dismissed. Pay attention to whether the relationship revolves around meeting the narcissist's needs while neglecting your own.

Understanding the narcissist's manipulation tactics is vital. They may employ gaslighting, distorting reality to make you question your perceptions. Take note of instances where facts are twisted or your feelings are invalidated. This manipulation can create confusion and self-doubt, eroding your sense of self.

Evaluate the impact on your emotional well-being. A relationship with a narcissist often leads to emotional exhaustion and a diminished sense of self-worth. Assess whether you find yourself constantly on edge, anxious, or feeling inadequate. Recognize the toll it takes on your mental health.

Consider the dynamic of control within the relationship. Narcissists often seek to dominate and control others to maintain their self-image. Reflect on whether you feel free to express your thoughts and opinions without fear of judgment or backlash. Identify power imbalances and whether your autonomy is compromised.

Assess the narcissist's ability to form genuine connections. While they may initially charm and impress, narcissists struggle with authentic emotional connections. Evaluate the depth of your emotional bond and whether it feels superficial or one-sided.

Explore patterns of behavior over time. Narcissists may exhibit a cycle of idealization, devaluation, and discard. Notice fluctuations in their treatment of you and whether your value seems contingent on meeting their expectations. Recognize patterns of manipulation and control that repeat throughout the relationship.

Consider seeking professional help. Narcissistic relationships can be emotionally draining and challenging to navigate alone. A therapist or counselor can provide guidance, support, and strategies for coping with the complexities of dealing with a narcissist.

Establish boundaries to protect your well-being. Clearly communicate your needs and expectations, and be prepared to enforce boundaries. Recognize that a narcissist may resist boundaries and attempt to manipulate or disregard them.

In conclusion, assessing a relationship with a narcissist involves a comprehensive examination of behaviors, emotional impact, power dynamics, and long-term patterns. Recognizing these aspects empowers you to make informed decisions about how to navigate the challenges posed by a narcissistic relationship. Seeking support from professionals and establishing healthy boundaries are essential steps toward safeguarding your well-being in the long term.

Moving Forward and Making Decisions

Moving forward in a relationship with a narcissist requires careful consideration and strategic decision-making to prioritize your well-being. Here are key aspects to consider:

Self-Reflection:
Begin by reflecting on your own needs, values, and boundaries. Understand the impact of the relationship on your mental and emotional health. Acknowledge any patterns of enabling or codependency that may have developed.

Acceptance:
Recognize that you cannot change the narcissist. Acceptance is crucial for making decisions based on reality rather than unrealistic hopes or expectations. Understand the limitations of the relationship and the likelihood of the narcissist changing their behavior.

Setting Boundaries:
To protect yourself emotionally, set up limits that are solid and unambiguous. Clearly communicate your limits regarding acceptable behavior. Be prepared for resistance from the narcissist, as they may try to push or disregard these boundaries

Seeking Support:
Seek assistance from loved ones, friends, or a therapist. Dealing with a narcissist can be isolating, and having a support system is vital. Share your experiences, feelings, and concerns with people you trust who can provide empathy and guidance.

Professional Help:
To negotiate the difficulties of the relationship, think about getting expert assistance. A therapist or counselor can offer valuable insights, coping strategies, and a safe space to explore your emotions. They can guide you in developing a plan for moving forward.

Evaluate the Relationship's Future:
Assess whether the relationship is worth maintaining. Consider the long-term impact on your mental health and happiness. Evaluate whether the narcissist is willing to engage in therapy or make genuine efforts to improve the relationship dynamics.

Exit Strategy:
If the relationship is toxic and detrimental to your well-being, contemplate an exit strategy. This may involve ending the relationship or, in cases of family ties or work connections, creating physical and emotional distance. Plan for potential challenges and seek legal advice if necessary.

Self-Care:
Prioritize self-care and focus on rebuilding your emotional strength. Engage in activities that bring you joy, pursue personal goals, and invest time in nurturing positive relationships. Cultivate a support network that encourages your growth and well-being.

Educate Yourself:
Learn more about narcissistic behavior and its impact on relationships. Understanding the dynamics can empower you to make informed decisions and navigate challenges effectively. An effective technique for empowering oneself is knowledge.

Forgiveness and Closure:
Work towards forgiveness, not for the narcissist, but for your own peace of mind. Recognize that closure may not come from the narcissist, and you may need to find it within yourself. Focus on letting go of resentment and moving forward with a newfound understanding.

Remember, moving forward is a gradual process, and it's okay to seek professional guidance to navigate the complexities of ending or restructuring a relationship with a narcissist. Prioritize your well-being and make decisions that align with your long-term happiness and personal growth.

Learning and Growth from the Experience

Experiencing a relationship with a narcissist can be emotionally challenging, but it also provides an opportunity for profound learning and personal growth. Here's a comprehensive exploration of the potential lessons and growth that can emerge from such an experience:

Self-Awareness:
The encounter with a narcissist prompts deep self-reflection. Through the challenges faced, individuals often gain a heightened awareness of their own needs, values, and vulnerabilities. Self-awareness serves as a basis for personal development.

Establishing Boundaries:
Dealing with a narcissist necessitates the development and reinforcement of boundaries. Recognizing the importance of setting limits becomes a valuable skill in all relationships, helping to protect one's emotional well-being.

Resilience and Strength:
Overcoming the manipulation and emotional strain inherent in relationships with narcissists cultivates resilience. Individuals learn to navigate adversity, building inner strength and fortitude in the face of challenging circumstances.

Enhanced Emotional Intelligence:
The rollercoaster of emotions experienced in such relationships fosters emotional intelligence. Learning to identify and manage one's emotions becomes crucial for maintaining stability and making sound decisions.

Empathy and Compassion:
Despite the lack of empathy in the narcissist, the individual on the receiving end often develops a heightened sense of empathy. Understanding the impact of hurtful behaviors fosters compassion for oneself and for others facing similar challenges.

Self-Validation:
The constant need for external validation from a narcissist prompts a journey toward self-validation. Individuals learn to recognize and appreciate their own worth independent of external approval, fostering a healthier sense of self-esteem.

Cognitive Flexibility:
Adapting to the ever-changing dynamics of a narcissistic relationship encourages cognitive flexibility. Individuals learn to navigate ambiguity, think critically, and adapt to unpredictable situations with resilience and creativity.

Improved Communication Skills:
Communication in narcissistic relationships is often
challenging. Learning to express oneself
assertively, while also actively listening, becomes a
crucial skill. Effective communication becomes a
cornerstone for healthier relationships moving
forward.

Prioritizing Well-Being:
The experience underscores the importance of
prioritizing one's mental and emotional well-being.
Individuals emerge from such relationships with a
heightened commitment to self-care and a better
understanding of the significance of overall health.

Forgiveness and Letting Go:
As individuals process the experience, they may
embark on a journey of forgiveness, not for the
narcissist, but for their own peace of mind. Letting
go of resentment and focusing on personal growth
allows for emotional freedom and closure.

Redefined Values and Priorities:
The challenges posed by a narcissistic relationship
often lead to a reassessment of values and
priorities. Individuals may discover a renewed
sense of purpose and direction, aligning their lives
with what truly matters to them.

In conclusion, navigating a relationship with a
narcissist, while undoubtedly challenging, can be a

catalyst for transformative learning and growth. The
lessons learned contribute to the development of a
more resilient, self-aware, and empowered
individual, capable of forging healthier connections
in the future. The key lies in extracting valuable
insights from the experience and channeling them
towards personal development and positive
change.

CONCLUSION

Dealing with a narcissist can be an intricate and challenging journey, requiring a delicate balance of empathy, self-preservation, and effective communication. As we navigate the complexities of relationships with narcissistic individuals, it becomes evident that understanding their behavior is crucial for establishing healthier dynamics. In this exploration, we've delved into the characteristics of narcissism, the impact on relationships, and strategies for coping and managing these challenging interactions.

 It is essential to acknowledge that engaging with a narcissist often necessitates a nuanced approach. Recognizing the signs of narcissistic behavior is the first step in safeguarding oneself from potential emotional harm. By understanding that narcissism exists on a spectrum, from subtle traits to a full-fledged personality disorder, individuals can tailor their responses accordingly. It's imperative to establish clear boundaries, maintaining a balance between empathy for the narcissist's struggles and prioritizing one's own well-being.

One fundamental aspect of dealing with a narcissist is cultivating self-awareness. Understanding one's own triggers, vulnerabilities, and emotional responses equips individuals with the tools needed to navigate challenging interactions. This self-awareness acts as a shield, preventing manipulation and emotional turmoil. In essence, maintaining a strong sense of self is a powerful defense against the subtle tactics often employed by narcissists.

Communication emerges as a pivotal factor in managing relationships with narcissists. Constructive communication involves expressing one's needs and concerns assertively while remaining open to dialogue. However, it is crucial to recognize that narcissists may resist acknowledging their own shortcomings. Therefore, managing expectations becomes paramount. Realizing that meaningful change in the narcissist's behavior is often limited allows individuals to make informed decisions about the level of investment in the relationship.

Setting boundaries is an indispensable aspect of dealing with narcissists. Establishing clear and non-negotiable limits helps create a safe emotional space. This involves being consistent in enforcing boundaries, even when faced with resistance or attempts at manipulation. By doing so, individuals signal that their well-being is a priority, fostering an environment conducive to healthier interactions.

It is crucial to remember that dealing with a narcissist can be emotionally draining. Seeking support from friends, family, or mental health professionals becomes vital in navigating the challenges posed by such relationships. Support networks provide validation, perspective, and encouragement, serving as a lifeline during moments of doubt or difficulty. Building a strong support system is an act of self-compassion, affirming that individuals do not have to face the complexities of dealing with a narcissist alone.

Self-care emerges as a cornerstone in managing relationships with narcissists. Prioritizing mental and emotional well-being involves incorporating activities that bring joy, relaxation, and fulfillment. Whether through mindfulness practices, hobbies, or engaging in positive social interactions, self-care serves as a counterbalance to the stressors inherent in dealing with narcissistic individuals. It is a proactive and empowering step towards maintaining resilience in the face of challenging dynamics.

In some instances, individuals may find that disengagement or limited contact with the narcissist is the healthiest option. While this decision is undoubtedly difficult, especially in familial or long-term relationships, it is an act of self-preservation. Creating distance allows for reflection, healing, and the possibility of establishing healthier boundaries in the future. It is crucial to recognize that choosing to step back from a toxic relationship is not a sign of weakness but a courageous decision to prioritize one's well-being.

In conclusion, dealing with a narcissist is a multifaceted process that requires a combination of self-awareness, effective communication, boundary setting, and self-care. Navigating these relationships demands resilience, compassion, and a commitment to prioritizing one's emotional health. By understanding the intricacies of narcissistic behavior and implementing strategies to mitigate its impact, individuals can foster healthier dynamics or, when necessary, make empowered choices to protect their well-being. Ultimately, the journey of dealing with a narcissist is a profound exploration of self-discovery, resilience, and the pursuit of emotionally fulfilling connections.